Children's Ministry Curriculum

I0129996

CHARITY SERIES
PRESCHOOL
BIBLE STUDY

DocUmeant Publishing

Published by
DocUmeant Publishing
244 5th Avenue, Suite G-200
NY, NY 10001

646-233-4366

Designed and formatted by Ginger Marks, DocUmeantDesigns.com

LCCN: 2024930469

ISBN: 978-1-957832-29-6

Course Program.

Lessons

SECTION

This section will explore biblical studies that will highlight the many ways in which God's love is demonstrative in the lives of biblical characters. It will also reveal how God is currently at work in extending His love to children as they are faced with life's most challenging situations. will also highlight the overall objectives and intended outcome of each lesson.

Page 1

Templates

SECTION

Section two provides the templates necessary to effectively complete each lesson. They are presented in numerical order coordinating with each lesson plan.

Page 57

David and Jonathan —A True Friend

Memory Verse

"You are my friends if you do what
I command you" (John 15:14).

Read: *A Friend in Need*

Tell me the name of your friend.
What do you like to do with your friend?
What makes your friend special to you?

In the Bible, it tells a story of a special friendship between David and Jonathan. David was the strong kid in the Bible who killed a lion and bear with a sling shot. He is best known for how he used three rocks to kill a big huge giant named Goliath.

When David had finished his job at defeating the giant, he went to work for the King. The king's name was Saul and he oversaw a lot of people. He had seen David destroy Goliath and wanted to give him a job in his army.

David thanked King Saul for the offer and went to work for him. He was also invited to stay in his home. While there, he met King Saul's son. His name was Jonathan. They became the best of friends. They also protected one another.

King Saul later became jealous of David because the people in the land, that he ruled over, liked David and respected him more than the King. This made King Saul so angry that he wanted to destroy David. His son Jonathan found out about it and did everything he could to protect David from his father.

Do you think King Saul should have been jealous of David? Was it okay for the King to want to hurt David?

What would you have done to help protect David from King Saul?

David and Jonathan continued to be close friends no matter what they had to face from other people. Now, this is a close friend. The Bible says a good friend loves at all times. So, no matter what, if you have a good friend treasure the friendship and always be good to one another.

How can you protect your friend?
What are some ways you can be good to your friend?

God also wants us to be His friend. He loves us more than our closest friend. When we obey God, we show Him our love in return.

You are my friends if you do what I command you" (John 15:14).

Remember, your friends are a blessing and a gift from God, so always be good and loving to your friends.

Prayer

Dear God,
Thank you for loving me. Thank you for choosing me to be your friend. Help me to show you love by my obedience to you. Thank you also for blessing me with special people in my life. I thank you for my family and my friends. Help me to treat both my family and friends with love and respect and to always treasure them.

In Jesus name,
Amen

Lesson One Activities*

Friendship Bracelets

Material needed

Assorted colorful beads

String

Friendship Puzzle

Give each child a puzzle piece to draw a picture of themselves. Connect all the pieces together.

See puzzle template "Lesson One: Puzzle Pieces" on page 57.

Friendship Tree

Draw a big tree. Use finger paint to paint each child's handprint on the tree.

Lesson 2
We Are God's Creation

"I praise you because I am fearfully and wonderfully made; your works are wonderful" Psalm 139:14 (NIV).

Read: *Loving the Skin I'm In*

In the very first book of the Bible, God uses Moses to tell His creation story. It only took God six days to create the world and everything in it. Everything that God created, He called it good. You and I were a part of what He called good.

When God went to work the very first day to create the world, He called forth the light. He used the light to brighten up a world that was very dark. This allowed us to have both day and night, and God said it was good.

The second day, God rolled back the water and placed a dividing line so that He could create a sky. This too He said was good!

The third day, God made an area to place grass, trees, and plants. He also made the sea, a place where sea creatures could live. And yes, He said it was good!

The fourth day God made the world a brighter place to live by placing a sun, moon, and stars to give more light during the day and late at night. This also was good God said!

The fifth day, God filled the sea with fish and other types of sea creatures. Afterwards, He filled the sky with all different types of birds. God declared, this was good!

The final day of creation, God did His best work. First He created all the animals on the earth. Then at last, He created man. But He was not finished yet. He realized that the man He created would be lonely, so, He put him to sleep, took a rib from his side and made a woman. God was very proud of His work that day and said it was very good!

Yes, we were God's very best work. He was proud of what He had made. Throughout the Bible, God made it known that humans were His special creation. He said that we were made in His image. God used His mouth to create the world, but He used his hands to create man and woman. Once his work was completed, he said that it was very good!

If God thinks, you and I are special, when we look in the mirror, we should always remember that we are precious in His sight.

What does say about His creation?
How many days did it take God to create everything?
How does God feel about you?
What should you think about yourself?

Prayer

Dear God,

Thank you for creating everything in this world for me to enjoy. Thank you for making me a special part of your creation. You created me in your likeness and you say that I am wonderfully made. Help me to see myself the way you see me.

In Jesus's name,
Amen!

Lesson Two Activities

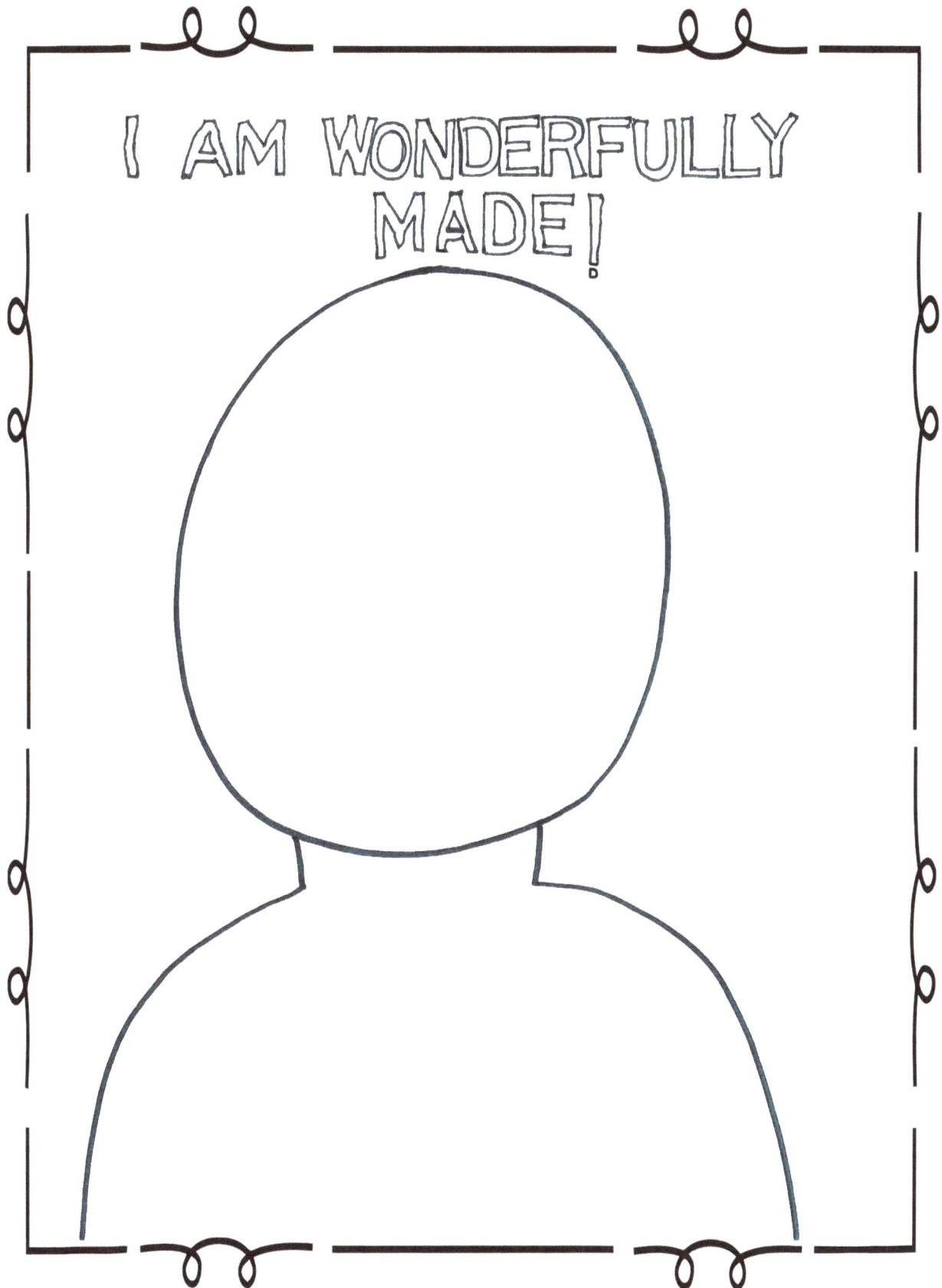

I AM WONDERFULLY MADE!

Mirror Activity

Material Needed

Handheld mirror or several mirrors

Mirror template see "Lesson Two: Mirror" on page 58

Tissue Paper

Glue sticks

Have each child look in the mirror and say one thing they like about themselves.

Use the mirror template and have each child draw a picture of themselves inside the mirror. They can color and decorate the mirror with tissue paper.

Write on it . . . I Am Loved!

You Matter!

Memory Verse

"Mankind, he has told each of you what is good and what it is the Lord requires of you: to act justly, to love faithfulness, and to walk humbly with your God" (Micah 6:8 CSB).

Read: *Your Life Matters*

Scripture: *Esther 1–4*

Today, we are going to learn about a special lady in the Bible. Her name is Esther. Esther was a beautiful girl. She was a Jew. Jews were God's chosen people whom He loved very much. Esther's family loved God and served Him faithfully.

When Esther was a little girl, both of her parents died. She was sent to live with her cousin Mordecai. He was very kind to her and raised her to believe in God. When Esther became a teenager she entered a beauty contest.

Esther won the contest. Afterwards, she was chosen by the king to be his bride.

The King was not a Jew. Neither did he know that Esther was a Jew. During this time the King had written a law that all Jews would be punished. This was not fair, so Esther decided to let the King know that she was a Jew. She begged the King to changed the law to protect her people. She did not want to see her people be mistreated.

The King decided to protect Esther and her people. God had placed Esther in the palace as the King's wife so that He could use her to protect His people. They mattered to God.

You matter to God and so do all His people. When you see someone being mistreated, always know that this hurts God's heart. He does not want anyone to be treated unfairly. Always remember that we make God happy when we treat people with kindness and justice.

Has there ever been a time in which you felt you were treated unfairly?
How does God want us to treat others?
When you see someone being mistreated, what is one thing you can do?

Prayer

Dear God,
Thank you for loving me and saying that I matter to you. Help me to be kind in my actions towards others. Also, help me treat others fairly. I pray that others will treat me and my family fairly too. Keep us protected from people who would want to mistreat us. Protect your people everywhere, especially those who love you and want to do your will.

In Jesus's name,
Amen

Lesson Three Activities

Sorting activity

Have pictures of kind and unkind actions from magazines or download images and make cue cards. (Minimum of five each.)

Discuss/Sort what's kind and what's unkind.

Give Me Five!

Trace each child's hand and have them tell you five words or actions for each finger.

Kindness Flower

Use Flower template "Lesson Three: Flower" on page 59 and have children glue the petals on the flower that list the following words.

Helpful
Loving
Patient
Caring
Kind
Polite respectful
Courteous
Sweet
Good

Encourage each child to do a random act of kindness.

Here's some suggestions:

Share one of your toys.

Hold the door for someone.

Write a kind note to someone or draw a picture.

Do a chore without being asked.

Say something kind to someone.

Donate old clothes or toy. (ask parents first)

Pray for someone.

Jesus Cares

Memory Verse

"... casting all your cares on him, because he cares about you" (1 Peter 5:7 CSB).

Read: *Sick & Alone*

Scripture: *Luke 8:49-56*

Today we are going to read a story in the Bible about a sick little girl. Her name is not known, but her daddy's name is Jairius. She was twelve years old and was very, very sick. Her daddy knew that Jesus had the power to make her well, so he left home to look for Him.

While the daddy was away, the little girl died. The people heard the news and went to tell Jairius. By this time, Jairius had already spotted Jesus in a crowd and asked Him if He could go home with him to heal his daughter. The people told him that it was

too late because his daughter had already died. Jesus felt sorry for this man, so He kept walking with him.

Jesus ignored the people and continued to head towards Jairius' house. Jesus told Jairius, if you believe, I will heal your daughter. Once Jesus arrived and saw the young girl lying on her bed, He spoke in a loud voice and told her to come back to life and she did. Jesus indeed raised this little girl from the dead.

Jesus loves and cares about us when we are sick. He uses our parents and the doctors to help us feel well again. He also sees and knows when we are in need of His help. He will always come to our aid when we are in need.

Prayer

Dear God,
Thank you for loving me and showing me care when I am in need. Thank you for always knowing when I need your help. You are a kind God and I thank you for all the times you heal me when I am sick. Help me to trust you to always be there for me.

In Jesus name,
Amen

Lesson Four Activities

Color the cross.

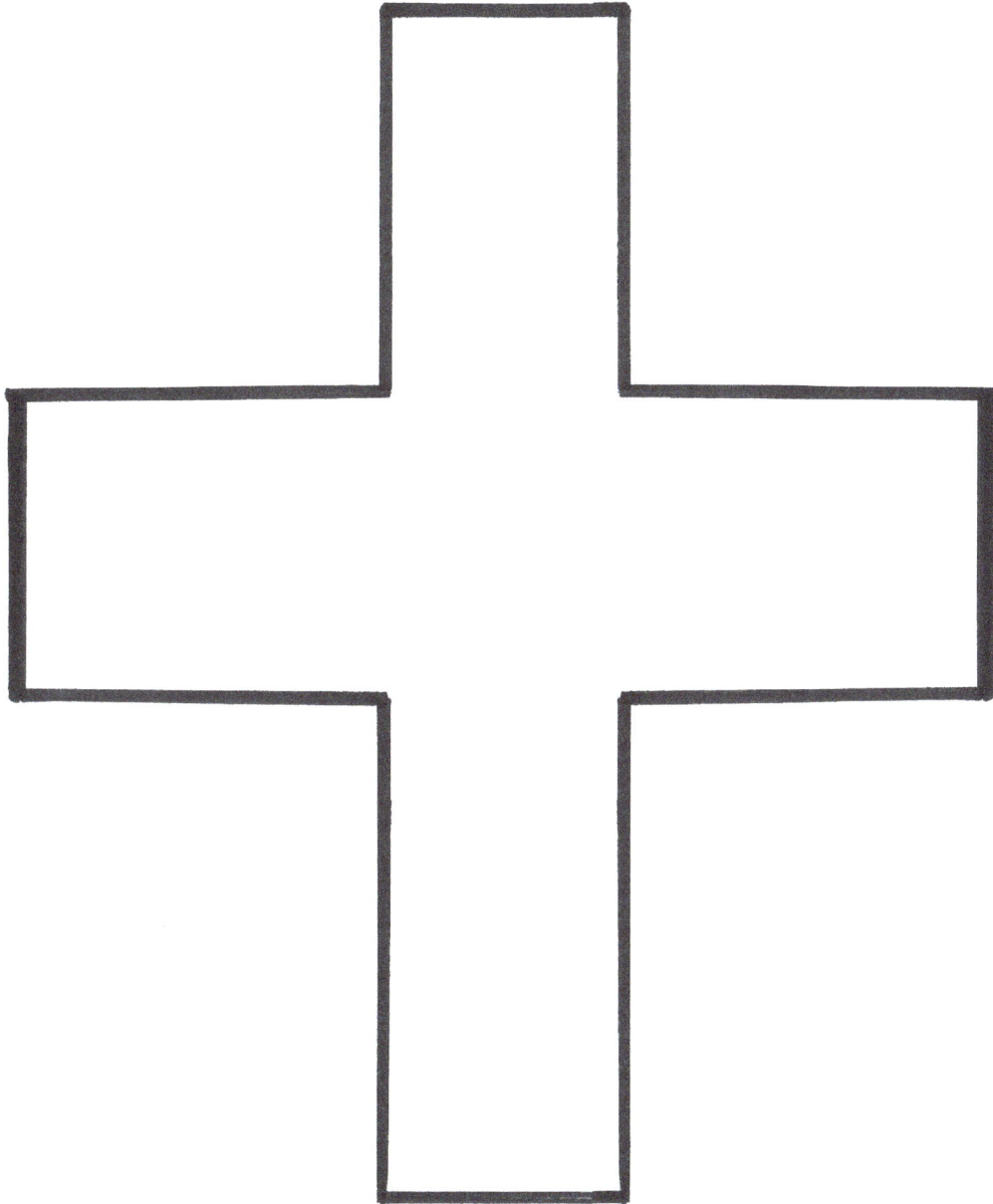

Cut out and fold the four hands template accordion style. See "Lesson Four: Wide and Deep" on page 61. Explain to each child how deep, high, wide, and long God's love is for them.

Teach them the song, *I've Got the Love of Jesus Down in My Heart*.

You Belong In God's Family

Memory Verse

"But to all who did receive him, he gave them
the right to be children of God, to those
who believe in his name" (John 1:12 CSB).

Read: *A Place to Belong*

Today we are going to learn about one of the most famous
people in the Bible. His name is Moses. When Moses was
born, there was a very mean King name Pharoah who ruled
the people. During this time, lots of people from Israel had
moved to Eygpt because there was no food in their land.
Pharoah made the people from Israel his slaves. He was
very mean to them and made them work very hard. They
were known as the Israelites.

Pharoah worked the Israelites all day and night. He began
to mistreat them too. Pharoah knew that if the people from

Israel had lots of babies, they would become powerful and take over his land. So, he made a law that if any boy babies were born by the Israelites, they would be thrown into the Nile river to be eaten by alligators.

One day, an Israelite lady had a baby boy. For some reason, she knew that her baby boy was very special. Instead of throwing him in the river, she decided to place him in a basket. She hid him in the river near Pharoah's house and kept her daughter nearby to watch over him.

Days later, Pharoah daughter was in the river and she spotted the basket. When she went over to look inside, she saw an adorable baby boy. She decided she would keep him and raise him as her own. Then she adopted him and

made him a part of her family. When Moses grew up, he became a very important leader to the Israelites, however, he remained grateful to Pharoah's daughter for being a good adoptive mom to him.

When we ask Jesus to come into our hearts, we become a part of God's family. He adopts us and calls us His children. We can depend on Him to be a good and loving Heavenly Father to each one of us, all the days of our lives.

Why did Moses' mom keep him hidden in a basket?
Who adopted baby Moses?

GOD ChoseU
John 15:16

What did Moses do when he grew up?

How can you become adopted into God's family?

Prayer

Dear God,

Thank you for being a good, kind, and loving Father. Thank you also for allowing me to be a part of your family. You make this possible when I invite you in my heart. As your adoptive child, help me to live my life so that I can make you proud of me. I want to be a good [son / daughter] to you.

In Jesus's name,
Amen

Lesson Five Activities

Decorate a Crown

Use template "Lesson Five: Crowns" on page 63 for crown, have each child decorate with beads or glitter.

Write each child's name on the crown.

Sing:

"Jesus Loves Me"
"Jesus Loves the Little Children"
"Father Abraham"

Treat Me With Love And Care

Memory Verse

"Jesus said, 'Leave the little children alone, and don't try to keep them from coming to me, because the kingdom of heaven belongs to such as these'" (Matthew 19:14 CSB).

Read: *Trouble at Home*

Scripture: "*I am the good shepherd. The good shepherd lays down his life for the sheep*" (John 10:11).

In the Bible, there is a story about a shepherd and his sheep. Have you ever seen a sheep before? Sheep are white woolly animals who live in green pastures or fields. Sheep are not very smart animals. They often wander away from the shepherd and get lost.

Did you know that sheep have enemies?

Wolves like to hunt for sheep. In order to keep the sheep safe from wolves, they need a shepherd. The shepherd's job is to protect the sheep and keep them safe. The shepherd will spend time looking for one lost sheep to bring it back to safety.

A good shepherd loves and cares for his sheep. He will never leave them unprotected.

Sheep know the voice of their shepherd. When the shepherd calls, a sheep will come in the direction of his voice. If a sheep chooses not to come, a shepherd will use his rod to bring the sheep back to safe pasture. If a shepherd has ninety-nine sheep, and one gets lost, he would leave the ninety-nine to find the one lost sheep.

Just as the shepherd loves his sheep, God loves little children. He is our shepherd and we are his sheep. His job is to provide us with loving parents who will take good care of us. If our parents mistreat us or do not take good care of us, God will not be pleased or happy with them. A good parent will always treat his / her children with love.

What is the job that God has given to every parent?
Tell me one thing a good parent does?
What shouldn't a good parent ever do?
How is a shepherd like a good parent?

Prayer

Dear God,
Thank you for being a loving Shepherd who takes good care of your sheep. Thank you for blessing me with a good parent, who takes good care of me. Help me to be a good child who loves and obeys my parent. Also, help me love and obey your voice as I choose to follow you.

In Jesus's name,
Amen

Lesson Six Activities

JESUS LOVES

Sheep Craft

Glue the sheep's head in the middle of a large white paper plate. Color the sheep's head black. Place cotton balls by glueing the cotton on the paper plate around the head.

Play Sheep, Sheep, Woof (like Duck, Duck, Goose)

Use the sheep's and wolf heads template "Lesson Six: Sheep and Wolf" on page 65 to create several sheep hats and one wolf hat.

Sit the children in a circle. Have one child outside the circle, be the wolf. The wolf will circle around the sheep. When one of the sheep is touched, they take off and run from the wolf. If the wolf catches the sheep before they make it around and are sitting in their original place, they become the wolf.

Kindness Always Win

Memory Verse

"Be kind to one another, tender hearted, forgiving one another as, God in Christ, forgave you" (Ephesians 4:32).

Read: *Don't Bully Me!*

Scripture: (Romans 8:32).

Today, we are going to learn about a man named Daniel. When Daniel was a teenager he was brought to live in a city called Babylon. He no longer had his family around to protect him. While Daniel lived in Babylon, he had to follow the rules of King Darius. The King was not like Daniel's old king. He had different rules, but Daniel was told to follow them. One of the rules was that Daniel had to eat certain foods. Another rule was that Daniel had to pray to the King's god. King Darius' god was not the same god that Daniel served.

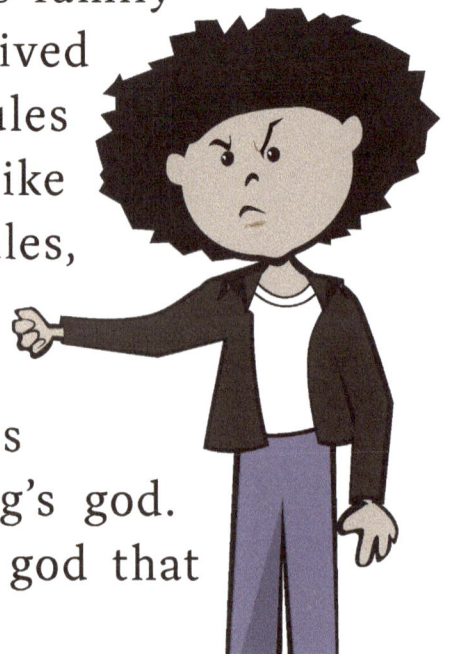

Daniel had a choice to make. He had to decide if He would obey the king and follow his rules or he could continue to obey his God and follow His rules. If Daniel chose to disobey King Darius, he would be thrown into the lion's den and eaten alive. This was a very hard choice.

What would you do?

Daniel decided to follow his God, so everyday he chose to kneel before his window and pray to God. He knew that if he ever got caught, he would become the lion's next meal. Daniel didn't care about the punishment because he loved his God and knew that He would protect him.

One day, some people spied on Daniel and he was praying.

What do you think happened?

The people went and told the King. Although the king liked Daniel, he had to keep his law. So, he had Daniel thrown in the lion's den. The lions were very hungry and wanted to eat him. But God protected him by sending angels to close the lion's mouths.

The next morning, King Darius rushed to see if Daniel had been eaten. Guess what? Daniel was still alive. The true God that he served protected him from being eaten by the lions.

The way that Daniel was treated was wrong, however, God protected him and kept him safe. If you are ever treated badly, pray to God and trust that He will send help your way to keep you safe.

What were the new laws that Daniel had to follow?
Why did Daniel choose to disobey the new laws?
What was Daniel's punishment for disobeying the laws?
What did God do to protect Daniel from the lions?

Prayer

Dear God,
Thank you for being the only true God. Thank you for always protecting me from people who may want to hurt me. Keep me safe and help me to always trust and obey.

In Jesus's name,
Amen

Lesson Seven Activites

KINDNESS

Cryptogram Puzzle

See "Cryptogram" on page 60. Using the key at the bottom solve the puzzle.

Create your own Charity

Color, cut out, heart and accordion arms and legs from template "Lesson Seven: Charity Accordion" on page 66 and place wiggly eyes to create your own Charity.

Materials Needed:

Cardstock paper
Large wiggly eyes
Foldable hands and feet

Fold the arms like accordians and attach to the heart. Decorate as you like.

The Easter Story

Memory Verse

"For God loved the world in this way: He gave his one and only Son, so that everyone who believes in him will not perish but have eternal life" (John 3:16 CSB).

Read: *The Easter Story*

(Sung to the tune of the Muffin Man)

Oh do you know the Easter story, the Easter Story, the Easter Story.

Oh do you know the Easter story about God's love for me.

It tells how Jesus died for me, died for me, died for me

It tells how Jesus died for me upon a rugged cross.

How many of you have heard the Easter Story?
What is Easter and why do we celebrate this holiday?
Why do we talk about Easter at church?

Today, we are going to learn about the true meaning of Easter?

Easter is not about bunnies and eggs. We used the bunnies and eggs as a symbol to welcome the arrival of Spring. Easter is really about an event that took place over 2,000 years ago. That's a long time ago, but we still celebrate it because it is one of the most important days in history.

At Christmas time we remember and celebrate the baby Jesus who came to us in a manger. This is also the beginning of the Easter story. God sent Jesus to earth because we were all so bad and we needed a Savior.

Jesus is the only perfect person and He was willing to be our Savior to save us from our sins. Because we were sinners, we needed someone who could take our sins away. God chose His only Son, Jesus, to die for each one of us, so that our sins could be forgiven.

When Jesus died on the cross, He took our punishment for sin and His blood was shed to make us good again. For this to work, Jesus had to come back to life.

It took Him three days to complete His job. He died on a Friday, but God raised Him from the dead early Sunday morning. Because He came back to life, we honor what He has done.

Easter is a time to celebrate that Jesus rose from the dead. His death was enough to erase our sin. When we ask Jesus to forgive us, His death on the cross makes us clean again.

Why did Jesus have to die?
What did His death on the cross do for us?

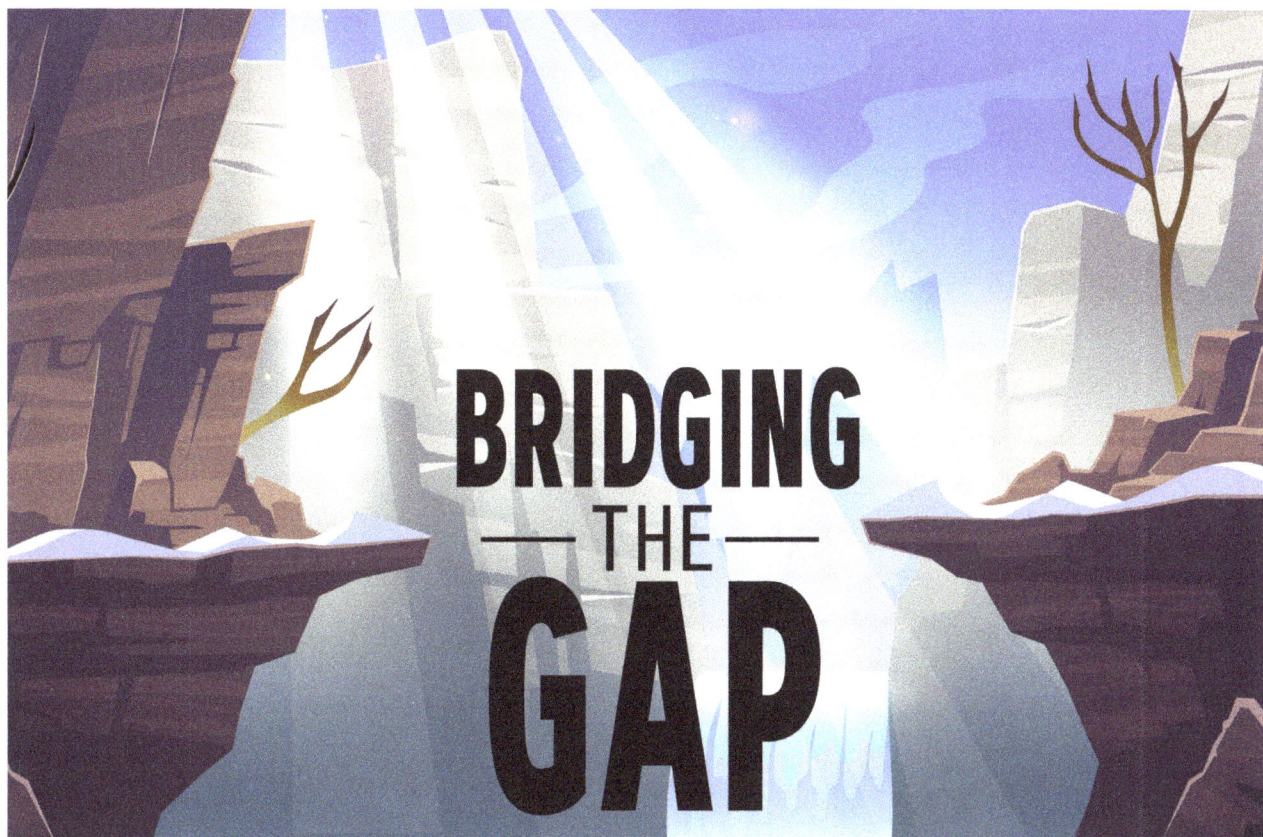

Would you like Jesus to come into your heart and forgive you?

Prayer

Dear God,
Thank you for sending your Son Jesus to die for me. I am so sorry for my sins. Please come into my heart and forgive me. Thank you for erasing my sin to make me good again. I give my life to you. Help me to do the things that please you.

In Jesus name,
Amen

Lesson Eight Activities

JESUS

SAVES

Tissue Paper Cross

Use color tissue paper to glue and cover the cross template. See template "Lesson Eight: Paper Plate Cross" on page 68

Paper Plate Easter Scene with Hands

Materials Needed:

One large paper plate
Green tissue paper
Construction paper
Watercolor paints
Paper glue

Use a half of one large paper plate and cover it with green tissue paper.

Trace both child's hands on construction paper.

Place the cross in the middle between both hands.

Have children paint the cross with watercolor paint.

Glue all parts together.

Honor Your Mom

Memory Verse

"Honor your father and mother" (Exodus 20:12).

Read: *Mom's My Shero!*

Scripture: *Proverbs 31*

Do you know who was with you when you first came into the world?

Do you know who heard you speak your first word?

Do you know who taught you how to talk?

Do you know who gave you your first meal?

Do you know who's there to hug and kiss you when you get hurt?

Who takes care of you and gives you everything you need?

The answer to these questions for most of you is your mommy. Moms are very special. They do so much to care for their little ones. They will put themselves last so they can put you first. They have a lot of jobs. They cook, clean the house, wash your dirty clothes, and take you where you need to go. They are your first cheerleaders. They also make you feel better when you are sad. They become a friend to you when you are lonely. When you're sick, they know how to make you feel better. Moms truly do love and care for their little ones. A mom is a child's first super-hero. Moms make the world a better place to live.

God knew that kids would need someone special to take care of them. So, when He created mom, He placed in her a lot of love, patience, kindness, forgiveness, and so many other things that would allow her to be that special person to take care of His little children.

God also chose a special mom to take care of His only Son, Jesus. Mary was her name. Without a mother, Jesus would not have been protected from the mean king who wanted to kill him when he was just a little toddler or pre-schooler like you. His mommy kept him safe and she also made sure He had clothes to wear, food to eat and a good home where He could feel loved.

You should always thank God for giving you a mom who takes such good care of you. You should also think about different ways to show your mom love and appreciation.

What can you do to let your mom know how much you love and appreciate her?

Prayer

Dear God,

Thank you for loving me and providing me with everything I need. Thank you for my mom and for all the ways she cares and provides for me. Lord, bless my mom and help her to know how much she is appreciated. Also, help me to always obey my mom and treat her with respect.

In Jesus's name,
Amen

Lesson Nine Activities

SUPER MOM

Handprint and Fingerprint Flowerpot with child's picture.

Mom's coupon book for five days

Have child come up with five ideas to use as a coupon for their mommy. See template "Lesson Nine: Coupon Book" on page 69

Examples:

1. Paint mommy's nails
2. Give mommy a back rub
3. Run mommy's bath water
4. Help with dishes
5. Bring home a good paper at school
6. Help fold clothes

Five Things I love about mommy handbook

Trace child's hand and cut out six hands out of construction paper. Title it on the front, *5 Things I love about Mommy.*

Have child tell you the five things for each page.

"I love mommy because ..."

Punch a hole on the side and tie it together with a ribbon.

Lesson 10

Our Heavenly Father?

Memory verse

"And my God will supply every need of yours according to his riches and glory in Christ Jesus" (Philippians 4:19).

Read: *Where's My Dad?*

Scripture: *1 Timothy 5:8*

In Luke 2 we read the story of the birth of baby Jesus. Before He was born, God picked a mommy and daddy for him. His mommy's name was Mary and his daddy's name was Joseph. God wanted two parents to raise His baby boy. He chose a mommy to give him hugs and to teach him everything about life. His daddy's job was to protect and provide for him.

Although mommies are important and they are always around, daddies are just as important as mommies in the life of children.

Just as God is a Father to Jesus, He is our Heavenly Father too. He looks from Heaven every minute of everyday to watch over each of us. He makes sure that all our needs are met. He also makes sure that we are protected and kept safe throughout the day and night. When are afraid, He wants us to know that He is right beside us. We are never alone. God loves us so much! He wants us to know Him. He also wants us to talk to Him. He has taught us a special way to talk to Him. This is called prayer. Here is one of the prayers that He wants us all to know. It is called the Lord's Prayer.

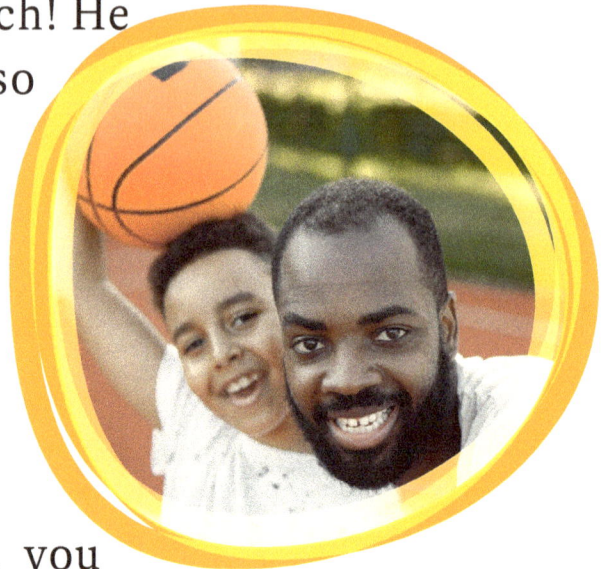

Charity and Champ will teach you how to pray the Lord's Prayer. It goes like this:

Charity: *Our Father, who art in Heaven,*

This tells us that God is listening and we should call him, Father!

Champ: *Hallowed be thy name.*

This tells us that the God we are praying to is not like anybody else. He is perfect and Holy, so we are to give Him praise.

Charity: *Thy kingdom come, thy will be done, on earth as it is in Heaven.*

This lets us know that God's way of doing things is best and we are to listen and obey His word.

Champ: *Give us this day, our daily bread.*

This tells us we are to ask God to give us everything we need and to also thank Him for everything.

Charity: *Forgive us our trespasses,*

We need to ask God to forgive us when we do wrong or make mistakes.

Champ: *As we forgive those who trespass against us.*

When others wrong us, we are to ask God to help us for give them too.

Charity: *Lead us not into temptation but deliver us from evil.*

We are to ask God to help us obey Him and make choices that make Him happy.

Champ: *For thine is the kingdom, the power, and the glory forever.*

This tells us great God is and we again give Him praise.

Charity and Champ: *Amen*

This means we agree and say yes to all that we pray in Jesus' name.

Lesson Ten Activities

Charity & Champ Puppets

See template "Chapter Ten: Charity and Champ" on page 71. Color and attach to large popsicle sticks. As each line of the Lord's Prayer is read out loud, have the children raise up either Charity or Champ.

Best Dad Award with Paper Plate
Material Needed:

Paperplate

Crayons or watercolor paint

Sticky stars

Markers

Hole punch

Ribbon

Use paper plate to make a medal for dad. Color or paint the outside ring and cover it with stars. In the center, write #1 Best Dad! See template "Dad Medal" on page 72. Attach ribbons to the bottom with ribbons. Holepunch holes for ribbons.

What's Heaven?

"In fact, we are confident, and we would prefer to be away from the body and at home with the Lord" (2 Corinthians 5:8).

Read: *Heaven Couldn't Waiit*

Scripture: *Revelation 21:1-4*

When you look up in the sky, what do you see?

Yes, there are clouds, rainbows, the sun, stars, and the moon. But there is so much more. We can't see it with our eyes, but way above the clouds, there is a place called Heaven. It is the place where God and Jesus live. We can't see them, but they can see us and everything else that happens in our world.

Heaven is the most beautiful place that God has ever created and one day we will all get to go and live there. God will have a special home for us to live there with Him forever.

Some of our loved ones are already there and they can't wait until we get there too. For us to go to Heaven, our life on earth must come to an end. This will only happen when God is ready for us.

God never wanted us to live here forever, so He created an even better place for His children in Heaven. In Heaven, we will never ever get sick, be sad, or get hurt. No one will ever say a mean word or hurt anyone's feelings. We will all be friends and love everybody. All the food will be yummy, and we will get to play and praise God all the time. It will be more fun than Dave and Buster's, Sky Zone, and even Disney World.

How will we get there?

There are only two ways to get to Heaven. The first way is for God to call us home when we die. The second way will be the special day that God has decided to come back

to earth to get all of His children. Either way, after this world, a greater world waits for us in Heaven. Heaven is a great place. To get into Heaven we need to love Jesus and live a life that makes Him happy.

Although, God may not be ready to take us to Heaven, we can experience Heaven on earth. God says in 1 John 10:10, "I came that you might have life and have it abundantly." (ESV) This means that God wants us to enjoy life on earth until He gets ready to call us to be with Him.

We can live a very happy life, but we will get sad, hurt, and even sick. Things won't always be easy, but we can trust God to help us and provide for us when we are in need. God promises to take care of us. So, when things get hard, call on God. He will be right there just when you need Him most.

Prayer

Dear God,

Thank you for preparing a special place in Heaven for me. I know you are not ready for me to go there yet, so until you do, please help me to live a happy life here. Also, remind me that you are always present with me to protect and provide for me. I love you! Help me to always serve you with all my heart.

In Jesus' name,
Amen

Lesson Eleven Activities

HEAVEN

Heavenly Mansions
Material needed:

Milk cartons, pop tart boxes, or other small boxes to use for creating mansions*

Glitter

Glue sticks

Assorted glittery beads

Metallic paint sticks

Assorted decorative craft paper (optional)

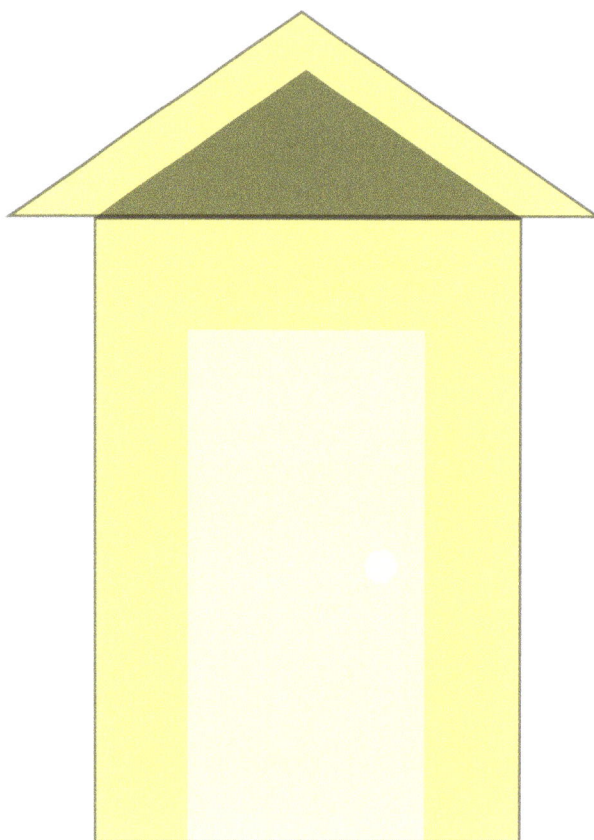

*If your carton has a cap make it into a chimney.

Charity Templates

Lesson One: Puzzle Pieces

Lesson Two: Mirror

Lesson Three: Flower

Cryptogram

Lesson Four: Wide and Deep

Cut out the cross and hands. Decorate as you like. Fold the arms like accordians and attach one to each cross stem.

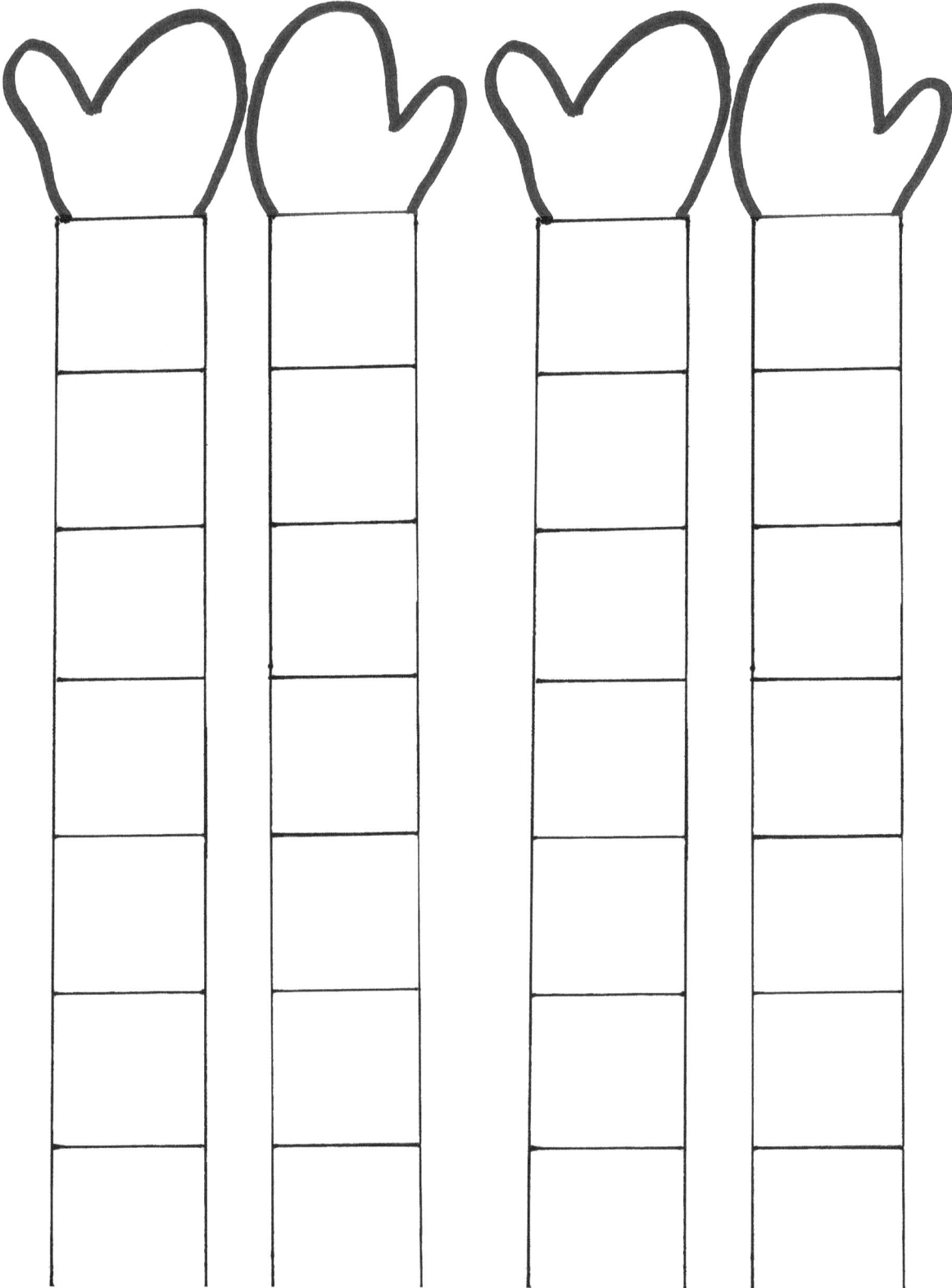

Lesson Five: Crowns

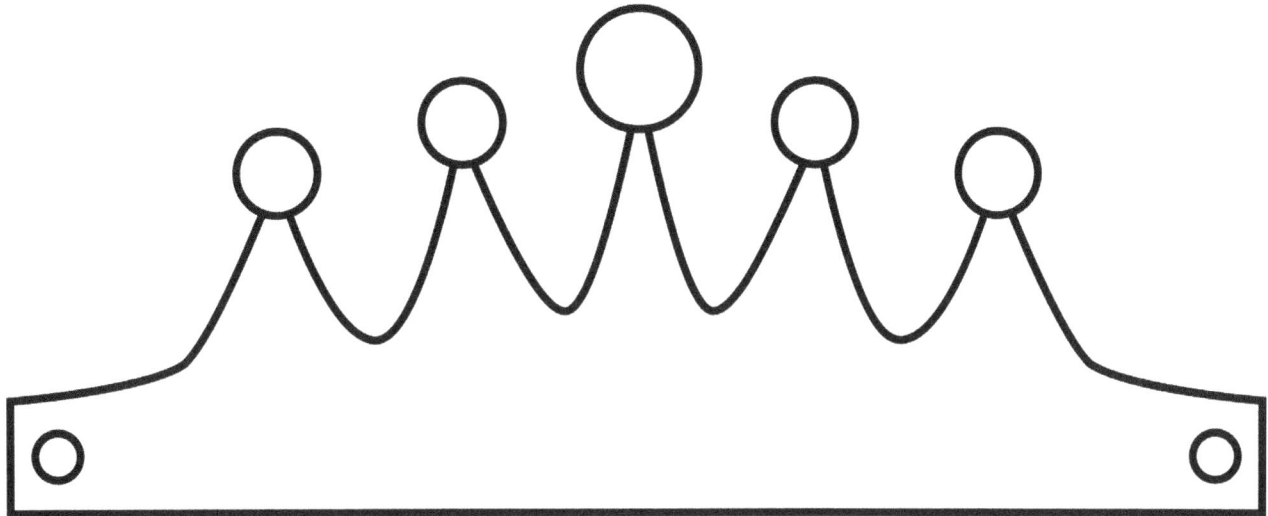

Spiritual Birth
Certificate

THIS CERTIFIES THAT

Has made the decision to invite Jesus to be Savior and is now adopted into the family of God.

DATE:

YOUTH MINISTER

PASTOR

Lesson Six: Sheep and Wolf

Attach each mask to a large popsicle stick with glue or tap

Lesson Seven: Charity Accordion

Cut out the heart shape, add facial features, and color it. Also cut out the arms and legs on the previous page. Fold the arms and legs like an accordian and attach to the heart with glue or staples to create your own Charity.

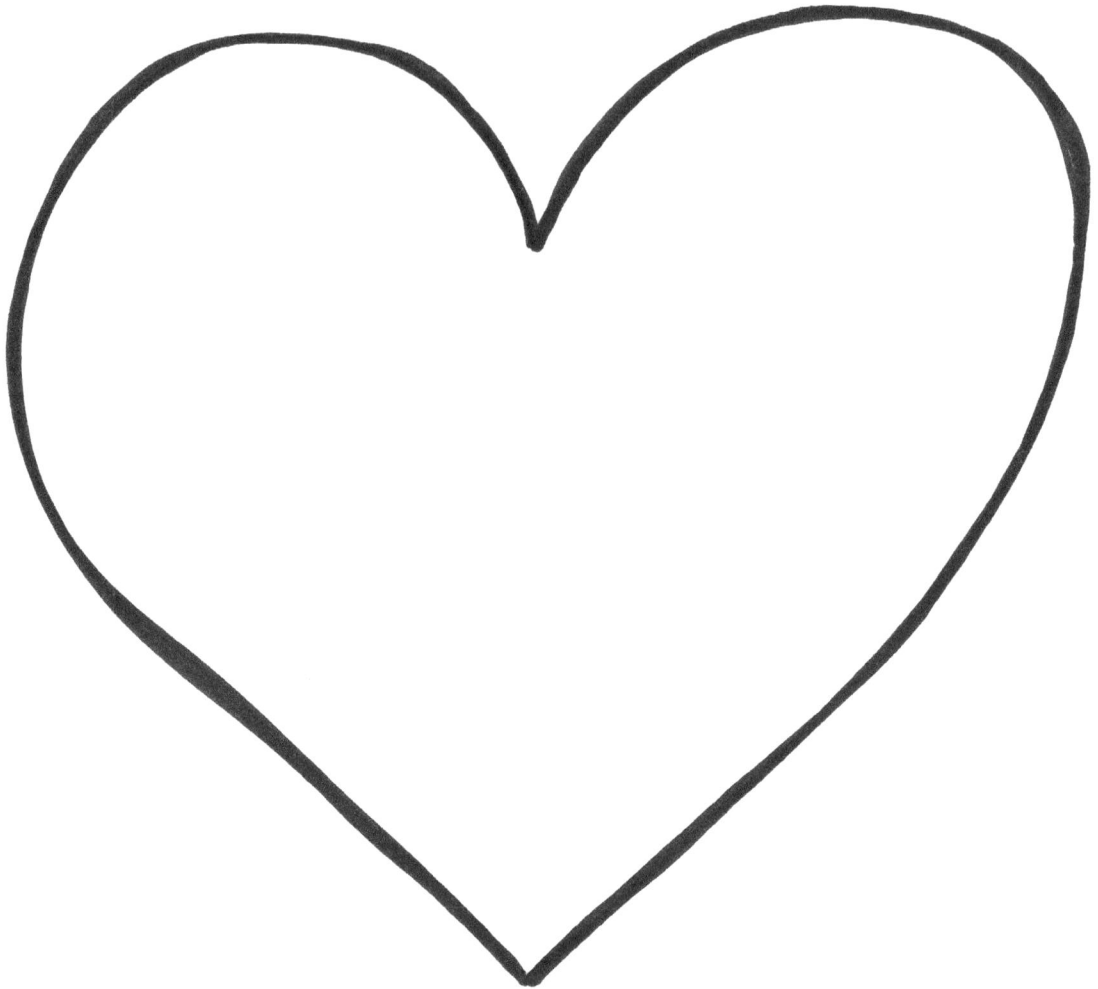

Charity legs and arms. Cut out and fold.

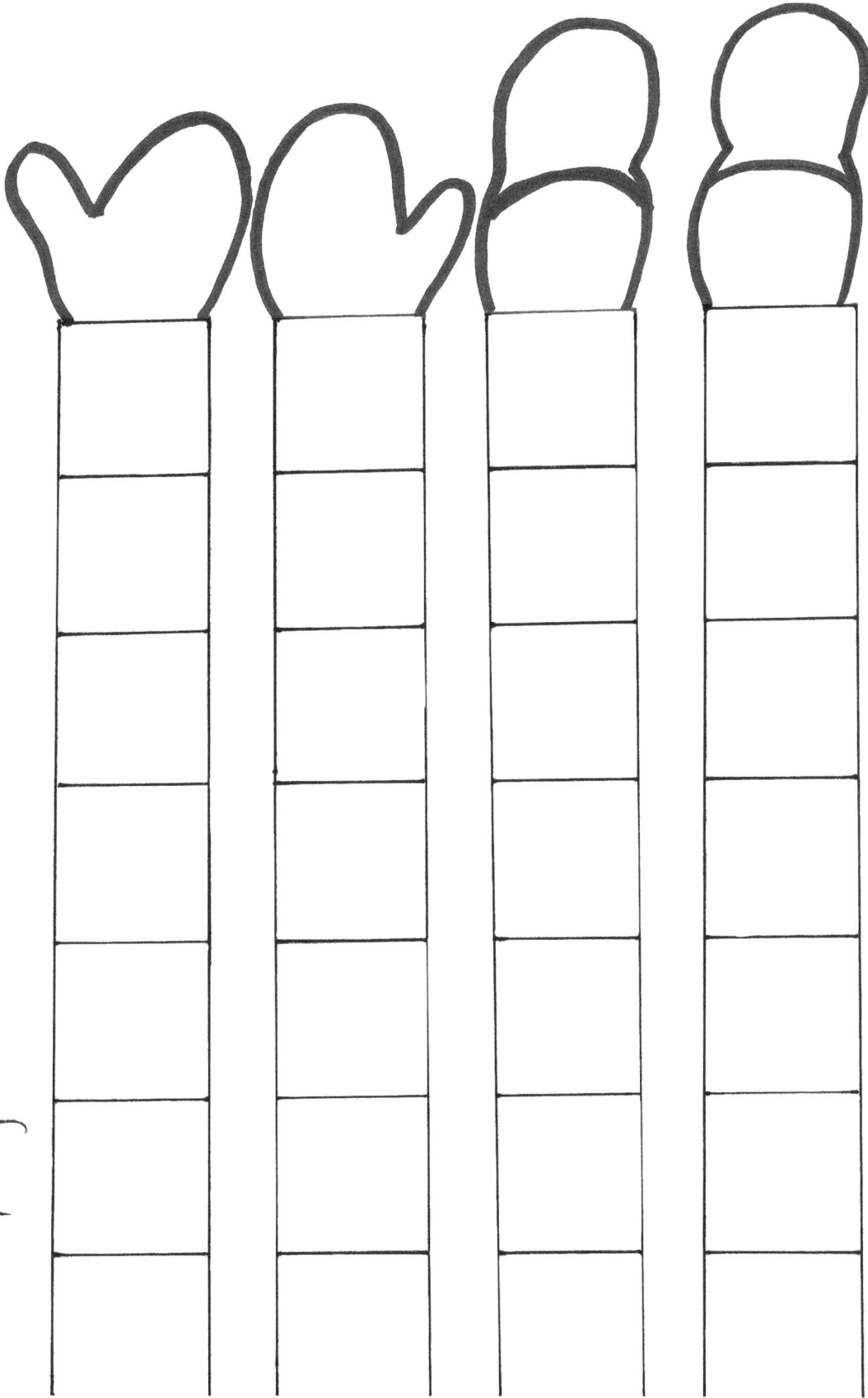

Lesson Eight: Paper Plate Cross

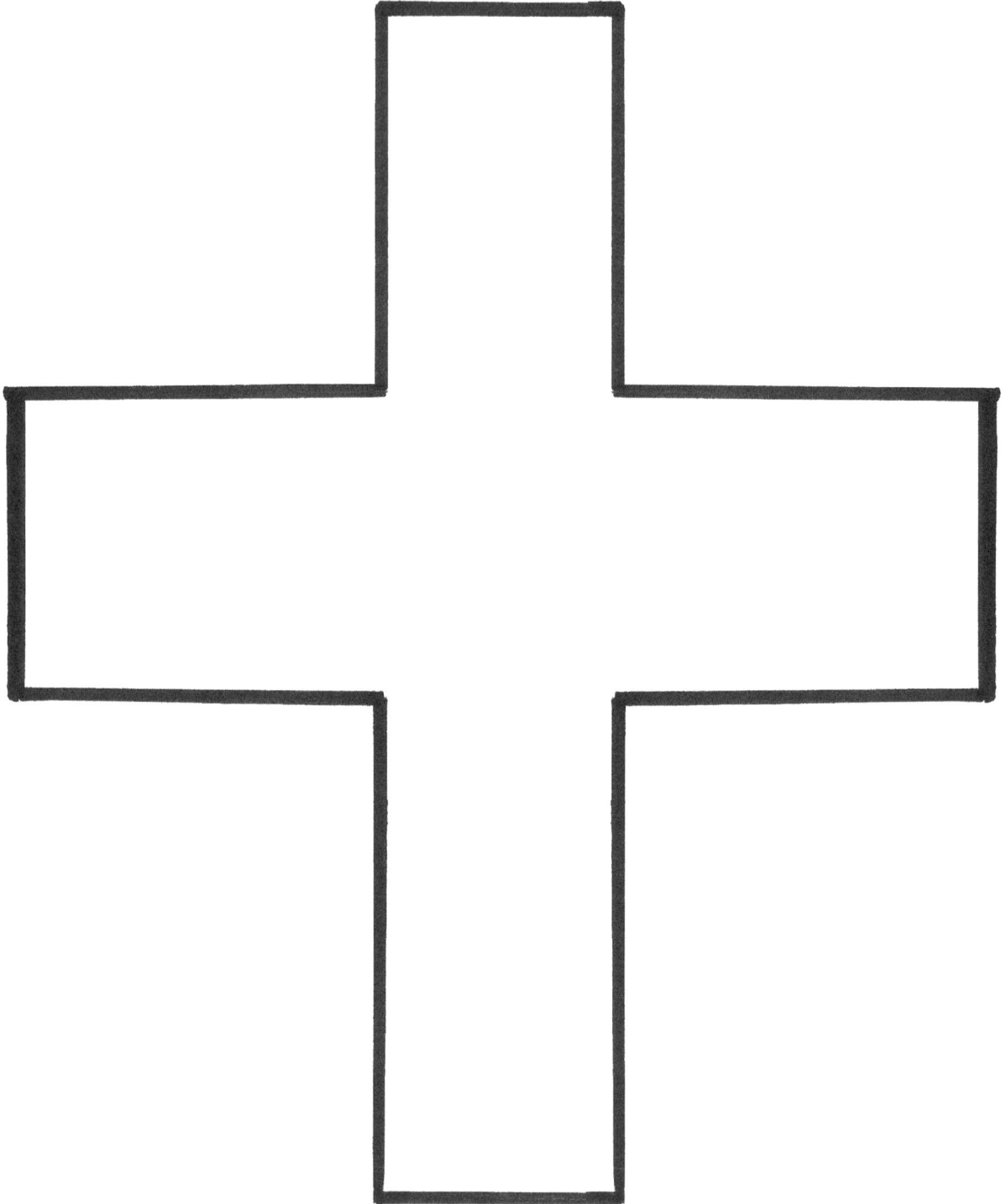

Lesson Nine: Coupon Book

Print out one cover and five coupons for each child.

Coupon Good for

Chapter Ten: Charity and Champ

Dad Medal

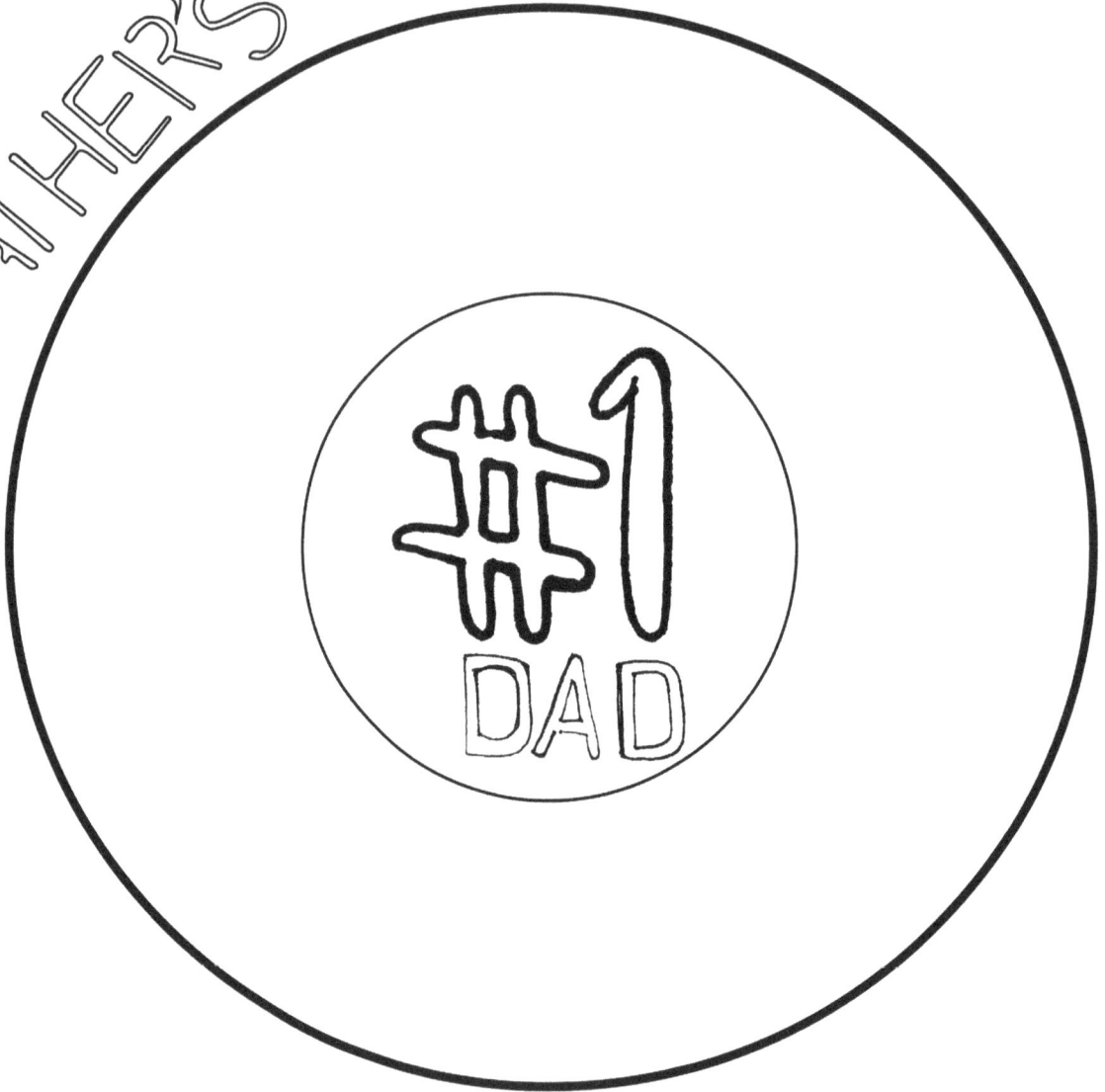

www.ingramcontent.com/pod-product-compliance
Lightning Source LLC
Chambersburg PA
CBHW061224270326
41927CB00025B/3492